Belief

The Foundation
To Success

PRAISE FOR BELIEF

"Mr. Gary Varnell is a man with insight and vision! In his new book *Belief, The Foundation to Success*, he connects with that inner voice that tells you, 'You can have success. You are a great leader and teacher.'

As a great leader, his book provides a clear vision of the great opportunity that lies before us when we fully commit and believe in ourselves. He unveils the truth that we can never outperform our own belief systems. But, just as important, he unfolds that vision in such a way as to generate enthusiasm and commitment. Leadership and vision are inseparable and Gary Varnell is the best at both!

His willingness to help others outpaces his desire for personal gain and those of us who have the good fortune to read *Belief: The Foundation to Success* are the benefactors of his passion, his wisdom and his experience."

-John E. Lang, President of Pinnacle Development

"The moment you meet Gary Varnell, you sense a powerful presence and depth. His belief in positivity and success is infectious and when you hear his story and what he endured to reach success, it is obvious that you want him to be part of your success journey. His book *Belief: The Foundation to Success* is a must read."

-Joe Courtney, Former NBA Player, Best-Selling Author and Speaker

"We have been blessed to work directly with Gary Varnell for the past seven years. We watched him achieve great success and attribute this to his hard work, commitment, determination, and belief that all things are possible."

-Jeremy & Mindy Deeble, Professional Networkers and Senior Vice Presidents of ACN

"Belief in myself and passion were instrumental in the success of my basketball career and my personal life. You always meet and experience special people along the way. That is why I allowed Gary Varnell to share a small portion of my story in his book *Belief: The Foundation to Success*. Gary Varnell captures the essence of what true success is in life. I agree with his theory that belief in yourself is your *first step* to true success. Winning shouldn't be the ultimate determinate of success, but it's important. No one wants to lose all the time. If you are going to commit to something and sacrifice for it and if you are going to apply yourself and work hard at something, you will find a way to achieve some level of success with strong belief in yourself. This is why without belief first, there is no success."

-Corey Yasuto Gains, Former NBA Player and Assistant Coach of the Phoenix Suns

"Gary is not only a friend, but has served as a mentor to me in my business life. He taught me that whatever your mind can conceive and believe, you can achieve. This book is a must read to open up the belief that everything is possible. Gary has demonstrated in his life that everything is possible and this book is a valuable resource to the possibilities to having your best life ever."

-Todd Stottlemyre, Former MLB Player, 3 Time World Series Champion and Entrepreneur

"I was very pleased when my friend Gary Varnell asked me to give my thoughts about life, determination and confidence for his new book *Belief: The Foundation to Success*. Life is all about believing in yourself and having goals. Mine, to be a professional athlete, was a long shot, seeing that less than a 100th of a percent of the population achieves that goal. That didn't stop me. It's easy to say it's too hard or impossible. But the ones who don't care about the odds, who aren't afraid to try and stick it out when it gets tough, are the ones who reach lofty status. Life isn't easy in any situation and it's important to believe in yourself; with hard work and maybe some help from friends and family along the way, life can go smoothly and can be less stressful. You can't be afraid of failure! Everyone in this world will fail at some point, most many times! The important part is to find solutions and the determination to keep trying. It's true, the statement that quitters never win and winners never quit. People don't like quitters. It's easy to quit, but the ones with the strong heart and a dream to be great usually find happiness where those traits bring them. No matter what your dream or goal is, have a plan and have the strength to never stop trying to achieve your goal. A friend of mine once told me, "Shoot for the moon! If you miss, you're still among the stars!" Not bad advice if you ask me.

-Jeremy Roenick, Former NHL Player,
Hockey Hall of Famer and NBC TV Hockey Analyst

"Mr. Gary Varnell is a man of high character and insight. In his new book *Belief: The Foundation to Success*, Mr. Varnell is spot-on about the key to success. Whatever a person believes is their reality; most people believe in their job more than they believe in themselves. In this powerful book, Gary will inform, educate and encourage the reader to tap into believing in themselves so they can have their ultimate success, dreams and goals!"

-Mr. Silas King III, Professional Networker

"Gary Varnell is a man who has demonstrated through his own life that the principles he shares will work if you work them. Through the years, I've come to know Gary as a dear friend and have witnessed firsthand that he is man of great purpose, passion and integrity. Gary's words will inspire you from deep within to fulfill your destiny and live your purpose."

-Larry DiAngi, Speaker and Author of *The Resilient Power of Purpose* **and** *Overcoming Rejection Will Make You Rich*

"Mr. Gary Varnell has pushed a button that will elevate anyone who reads his book. Setting goals and realizing dreams is a simple process if you travel the correct road. Gary puts you on the road and drives you right to success with his new book *Belief: The Foundation to Success!*"

-Eddie Johnson, Former NBA Player Phoenix Suns and Television Announcer

"I've always had respect for people that have a balanced life. Gary is one of those individuals that has proven that you can be successful and at the same time have a balanced life. He is always positive and looking to help others conquer more. He is a remarkable gentleman! His book on belief brings to the reader ideas and plans on how to create success. Belief is the motor of success! Without belief there is no power to drive towards your dreams."

-Mathieu Lamontagne, Professional Networker and Senior Vice President of ACN

"I've known Gary Varnell for several years and was happy to share my thoughts on belief and success for his new book. In the Latin, confidence literally means "with faith." In order to achieve what you want out of life, you must be confident. And as it relates to following your passion and utilizing your strengths, you must demonstrate self-confidence – faith in yourself.

-Chris Widener, Author of *The Art of Influence*

"I had the very fortunate occasion to meet Gary through a mutual friend. It is his nature to encourage and mentor and I have been the beneficiary of his natural ability to encourage those around him to believe in themselves based on his passionate belief that we all can achieve more if we just tap into that same emotion. It has been my personal experience that most people for some reason move through life in neutral. When you believe passionately in something bigger than yourself, people will respond if for no other reason than they desire to have that same conviction. Gary helped me define my own mantra and belief: no matter where you have come from and what life you have led – whether you believe your best days are behind you or in front of you – you will be correct."

-Norm Fitzgerald, Senior Vice President, National Field Sales, National Mortgage Insurance Corporation

"I have been fortunate enough to have known Gary Varnell for the past 12 years and knew from my first introduction that he was the kind of individual I wanted as a friend for life. What I can say from my heart is that Gary is absolutely one of the most positive and happy individuals I have ever had the pleasure of knowing! He exemplifies what it is to be a good human being and he does this with a belief system that sets him apart from most. That is why he is so likeable, so approachable and so successful. And to know the challenges Gary overcame in his youth suggests that he can relate to so many of us, both those who were given a chance and more importantly, those who may have been less privileged. If you haven't been as fortunate as me to know Gary personally, and you are looking for the key to finding success from within yourself, then I highly recommend you get to know him through his book, which speaks to those who want to get more out of life and to believe in themselves like no other. I am so happy that Gary is able to share so much to so many through his words."

-Ronald L. Ginter, ChFC,
Personal Financial Advisor for Ameriprise Financial

In "Belief: The Foundation to Success", Gary Varnell reveals the central truth behind personal achievement. In my experience having led thousands of financial advisors throughout my 30 year career, I can say with confidence that the key to success is a fire in the belly kept alight by a strong faith in one's ability to do the hard work. This is an inspiring read, well worth the time.

-Kim Webb, General Partner, Edward Jones

Belief:
The Foundation
To Success

Gary L. Varnell

Made for Success
PUBLISHING

Made For Success Publishing
P.O. Box 1775 Issaquah, WA 98027
www.MadeForSuccessPublishing.com

Distributed by Made For Success Publishing
Consulting Editor: Amber McClendon

First Printing
Library of Congress Cataloging-in-Publication data
    Varnell, Gary
    Belief: The Foundation of Success
    p. cm.

        ISBN: 978-1-61339-854-8
        LCCN: 2015916820

        Printed in the United States of America

For further information contact Made For Success Publishing
+14255266480 or email service@madeforsuccess.net

CONTENTS

ACKNOWLEDGEMENTS

F irst I want to thank my wife, Donna Lynn Varnell, for her love and support. Without her support my dream to write this book and to pursue my passion of public speaking would not have been possible. She helped me tremendously with creating the title and by suggesting ideas and changes to make the book better. Donna is the love of my life, my best friend and soul mate. She makes me a better man.

Thank you to my daughter, Amber Lynn McClendon. Amber and I sat for hours discussing content and she helped me formulate my ideas for this book. I wanted to spend time with Amber and help her reach one of her goals in life, which is to become a published author. We are doing this together so she can learn how to create her own success.

I want to thank my son, Brandon Varnell; he has written and self-published several books and helped me to get started with publishing this book.

Greg Provenzano, I wanted to thank you for your leadership and your personal mentorship. What I have learned from you helps me be a better husband, business professional, leader, speaker and mentor to others.

Jeremy and Mindy Deeble, thank you for your mentorship, friendship and support in my MLM business and in my personal life.

I also want to thank you for allowing me to share your story of success and belief in this book.

Thank you to my friend, John Lang, for allowing me to interview you and share some information about your road to success. You have always been supportive of me and have inspired me to move forward on this project.

I want to thank my friend, Todd Stottlemyre, for allowing me to tell a small segment of his success story. I also want to thank him for his inspiration and confidence in me to move forward with this book and public speaking.

I want to thank my friend, Corey Yasuto Gaines, for allowing me to share his road to success. Corey and I shared a similar background and road to success.

Sherrie Sampson and Michael Campbell, thank you both for being so supportive and such good friends of Donna's and mine. Thank you for sharing some excellent ideas to add to this book in order to make it more impactful.

Larry Raskin, I wanted to thank you for your mentorship on mental toughness and on leadership. You have had a big influence on my life personally and professionally.

I also wanted to thank Cavalier Franco LoFranco for the time you spent with me mentoring me and sharing your wisdom on personal growth.

Thank you to Lou Burgess for giving me quotes and advice on the book and on public speaking.

And most of all, I want to thank my mother and father, Betty June Varnell and John Henry Varnell. My success in life is in part based on what I learned and experienced through them. I am the man I am today, because of their love, support and belief in me. They instilled many of the success principles in me, even though they didn't really know these principles on a formal basis. They learned them from their personal application in life.

MY LIFE PHILOSOPHY

"Be grateful for what you have in life but don't settle for it! Be happy with who you are, but don't get too comfortable. To have more in life and be more in life, you must believe more to become more; then you'll do more, which means you'll have more."

PREFACE

My goal with writing this book is to change your way of thinking so you can improve your level of success in life. This book has been written to help everyone develop more belief in themselves and therefore have more success in their lives. This book will encourage you to find your purpose and your dream. By sharing solid principles and real life examples, this book will show you there is no limit to what you can have and what you can accomplish.

I will share ideas, other success stories, and the application of these principles. These examples and your application of these principles will assist you in achieving your own successes in life. Above all else, you will understand why belief is the one thing, the main thing you must have to create your success. These time proven principles will not work for anyone without belief. I will share why belief is so important and why belief is necessary in order for all the other principles to work to their maximum capacity for you. We will talk about different beliefs structures from belief in yourself (self-confidence) to belief in your vision, company, product, business, and even in life. Belief above everything else is the 1st building block on your foundation of principles to success.

I finished writing this book in the summer of 2015. As of 2015, for the past thirty-five years, I worked in corporate America in sales, national account sales, sales management and training, human resources, as a chief operating officer (COO), and in business for myself. During that time I've had extensive, leadership, sales, personal growth, and success training. I've read hundreds of books on these subjects. I've attended hundreds of hours of seminars on these subjects. I've trained thousands of people on these subjects and principles, from my own personal experience, personal application, readings and trainings. I'm very excited to share this information with all of you. I want this book to make an impact on your life.

CHAPTER ONE
IDEAS ABOUT SUCCESS

S uccess is something that anyone can achieve if they follow proven success principles. One of the most important factors in creating success is not just following and applying proven success principles, but having the right mindset. You need to make positive changes in your thought process and mindset to accomplish success. There are several attributes and basic success principles every individual must apply to create their own success. In this book, everything you need to know, apply in your life and believe will be revealed through real life examples. So, if you choose to create the life you desire, you can create that success for yourself. Here is a key: if one person can have success in life, then so can another person, as long as they have the attributes needed, put in the effort necessary and apply the success principles. Success starts with *belief*. Belief in yourself and belief that you can and WILL create the success you are striving for.

- Is your desire strong enough?

- Is your vision or goal crystal clear?

- Is your vision or goal written down?

- Do you have a step by step written plan to accomplish your vision or goal?

I want to share some background on how the mind works. Everything we do starts with a single thought. In a book titled, *The Book on Mind Management*, author Dennis R. Deaton writes, "The consummate truth in life is that we alter our destiny by altering our thoughts. The mind is our most crucial resource, our crowning asset, our ultimate arena of battle. If we will master the power of our minds, we may do or be whatsoever we will." Here is a simple example: if the thought is "I'm hungry," the mind creates a plan of action. The action you take from that thought is to get up, go to the refrigerator and find something to eat. It's the same with creating success. If you believe in yourself, you believe you can create your dream of success. Your mind will then formulate a plan to take action and move forward toward accomplishing that thought or goal. If you don't believe in yourself and you don't think you can create and accomplish your dream, your mind will not work to create a plan. You have already quit on your dream because you don't believe you can create it and live it.

Often times these negative thoughts come from an individual's lack of self-worth. At times people don't feel they deserve more than what they have. If this is your thought today, my hope is that this book will change your mind. It is my belief that anyone can create and live their dream. This book shares true life story examples of how to do this by using the proven success principles and acquiring and or developing certain characteristics; anyone can have success if they really want it and BELIEVE that they can and will have it. Dennis R. Deaton from *The Book On Mind Management* says "Change your thoughts, and you change your world. It all begins in the mind."

- Do you feel you deserve your dream, vision or goal?

- Do you have doubts about yourself?

- Do you have doubts about your abilities to accomplish your vision, goals or dreams?

The success principles we will go over in this book that are necessary are as follows:

- **Belief** – a strong desire to create and have your dream become a reality.

- **Vision** – being clear on your goals, dreams, and desires and writing them down.

- **Strong work ethic** – creating great success takes great effort.

- **Integrity** – being true to your word at all times, being honest in your dealings.

- **Commitment** – continuing to pursue your dream long after the feeling has left you.

- **Persistence** - a willingness to search out the information needed to create your success; a willingness to do whatever it takes to make your dream a reality.

- **Excellence** – doing your best with your appearance, your health, and your work.

- **Affiliations** – creating your success with the help of others; choosing your affiliations well.

To create your ultimate success there will be sacrifice involved. You will also need to create a step-by-step, detailed action plan to follow. This book will share ideas on how to accomplish that success. First and foremost you need to decide specifically on the dream, life, or goal, that you want to create. It never ceases to amaze me that people will spend countless hours researching a purchase of a refrigerator or a washer and dryer, new golf clubs, where they want to vacation, but when it comes to their dream, their goals, their life, no one really takes the time to think about it, or plan for it. Benjamin Franklin once said that some people die at age 25 and aren't buried until 75. Meaning our dreams, our vision, and our hopes can die so young. Once we jump into the work force, we come to the realization that we are working paycheck to paycheck for the rest of our lives. Do not lose hope. Recreate and hang onto your dream. Someone out there, right now, is living the life you want. If they can, you can too.

- Are you willing to take the time necessary to develop your vision, goal or dream?

- Are you willing to develop a written plan to accomplish your success?

- Are you willing to evaluate what you are currently doing and change it if necessary to work on the most important things first?

PERSPECTIVE AND BACKGROUND

Based on my work experience, personal experience, and working with thousands of individuals just like you, I finally came to the realization that the one thing missing from the people that have had some success, but remained only average, was the lack of a strong belief and vision of the success they wanted to create. The lack of belief and vision kept them from creating their ultimate success. You must believe in yourself. You must have belief that you deserve the success you want in life. To have huge success with your job, you must have belief in your company, product or service. Without belief, the time-proven principles of success will only grant you mediocre success. Your success will level out at your level of belief.

Here is the question I pose, and will answer in this book by the end: why are some people successful, while other people are not? I'm not sure if you have ever thought about this before. If not, it's time you did. That question is a very interesting question, don't you think? I've thought about it a lot and that is why I've written this book. I personally feel that each and every person that truly believes that they deserve success, applies the principals of success, works hard enough, long enough and effectively enough can and will create the success they desire.

I want to give you some perspective. Let's go back to the question. Why are some people successful while other people are not? Think about it! If you look at a group of people in a high school or college graduating class, anywhere in the world, after ten or twenty years, some of these people will have created great success while eighty to ninety percent of them have not. Why? What makes the top 3%, 5%, or 10% the top 3%, 5%, 10%? Do they have a vision of the desired success? Do they believe fully that they can achieve the success? Do they believe in themselves? Do they work harder? Do they set goals? Do they create a plan to achieve those goals? Are they more persistent? Are they consistent? Are they committed to their vision? Do they fight through adversity or do they quit short of their goals? Do they strive for excellence in everything they do? The answer is they do all these things and more at a higher level.

In my experience, the biggest difference between the ultra-successful people and everyone else is their belief level. It is their level of belief in themselves, in their business, project or company. These top money earners have a clear vision that they will have success and that they deserve that level of success. Successful people expect to have success. Average people say, "I'll give it a try and see if it works out for me."

It is my opinion that the one area of belief above all the others is self-belief and belief that you deserve success. If you don't believe in yourself and you don't believe you deserve the success, your mind will never develop the plans to achieve your vision or dream of success. You have basically said to your subconscious that you don't deserve it so you don't believe it will happen. Your mind then says you can't accomplish the vision and shuts down. Now you have a dream without substance. It will remain a wish or dream instead of a goal with a plan. I'm not a psychologist, but I've read many books on the mind and how it works. Here is a very simple explanation: everything you do, every action, every move you make, starts with a single thought. Earlier I shared this example: if your thought is "I'm hungry," you'll get up, go to the refrigerator and find something to eat. If your thought is, "I cannot succeed, I could never be a millionaire, I could never be promoted at my job," you are right. Your mind, based on that negative thought "You can't," will never create a plan to accomplish those goals. On the other hand, if your thought is, "I will be successful. I will be a millionaire. I will get that promotion," you are also right. Your mind will then start the process to create ideas, plans, and the action necessary, to reach the goals that you believe in and believe you deserve. In the final analysis, whatever you focus your thoughts on, your *dominant thought*, is what your mind will plan and create. Whether positive or negative, your mind will carry out whatever you are focusing on.

- What thoughts are you focusing on?

- What are your goals?

- What is your vision of success professionally, financially, personally?

- Are your thoughts positive or negative?

It is very important to remember that your conscious mind can only focus on one thought at a time, positive thought or negative thought. It is very important that you keep your focus on the positive side as much as possible. Think thoughts like, "I can accomplish this and I will make this happen." Larry DiAngi, in his book *Overcoming Rejection Will Make You Rich,* states that we have 40,000 to 50,000 thoughts daily. Of those thoughts, for most people, 87% are negative thoughts while only 13% are positive thoughts. That means we have between 34,800 and 43,500 negative thoughts daily. That is a staggering statistic. If we change our thinking and work to think more positively, even just a little bit, it will have a huge impact on our success. Your thoughts are your choice.

- Are you grateful for your job or do you hate it?

- Are you grateful for the home you have or do you wish you had a better one?

- Are you grateful for having a car to drive or do you despise getting in it every day?

- Change your thoughts and you can change your outcome.

Another perspective I want share, prior to discussing belief and the other success principles, is taking **responsibility for where you are in life.** This is a must to move forward and create the success you deserve and desire. Everyone, and I do mean everyone, must understand and take responsibility for where they currently are in life. We cannot move forward without doing this. We are all right where we are supposed to be based on the choices we have made in life. Here are examples of what I'm talking about. We choose to go to college or not. We choose to work a certain job or not; we choose to stay at that job or move on somewhere else to a new job; we choose how much effort and time we put into that job to have success. Where we currently live is based on the choices we've made. The car we drive is also based on these choices.

Until you are ready to take full responsibility that you are where you are in life based on your choices, you cannot and will not move forward in life toward success. You can't blame your parents; you can't blame your teachers; you can't blame your boss; you can't blame your coaches. It's all about you and the choices you have made in life. It's not about the adversity you have faced. It is about how you choose to handle that adversity. In fact, everyone faces adversity and problems in their lives. The difference between ultra-successful people and those not as successful is how the ultra-successful people choose to handle the adversity and problems. The fact is, the more successful a person is, the more adversity they have faced and the problems are bigger that they have had to overcome.

- Are you willing to take responsibility for the choices you have made in life?

- Are you willing to take responsibility for where you are in life based on the choices you have made?

- Are you ready and willing to make a different choice today so you can be in a better place tomorrow?

LIFE LESSONS

You must believe that success is something that everyone can achieve. We have been talking about specific success principles and laws that if followed, will produce success for anyone. How far up that ladder of success an individual goes is determined by how strongly they believe in themselves, how clear their vision of success is, how strongly they want to succeed and how hard they work at the principles of success. Some of the attributes necessary to be successful are belief, desire, work ethic, commitment, positive attitude, personal growth and seeking wisdom, taking personal responsibility, excellence, creating a plan, and taking action on that plan consistently and persistently over time.

Everyone in life has ups and downs. Everyone has trials in their lives that challenge them. Everyone has tragedy in their lives. Successful people have these ups and downs too. The difference is how successful people handle them. They don't allow these challenges to get them off track. They stay committed to their dreams and goals. Have you ever seen someone living in the house of your dreams? Have you ever seen someone in your dream car? Have you ever seen someone living the lifestyle you want? Why is it that their dreams came true and yours haven't? The people that are living their dreams are doing so because they have lived by proven success principles. By creating a step by step plan, they turned their dream into their reality. If they can live their dream, why can't you?

We are where we are in life because of a series of choices. Our choices are based on our individual perspective. Perspectives can be based on where we were raised, the environment we were raised in and who we hung out with. It's also based on our belief system in ourselves. There are a few exceptions to this rule, like someone whose father owned a company and they simply took it over; they didn't really climb to success, they were merely handed their place in life. If that's not you, then it is time to change your thinking and choose a different direction for your life.

Here is the beauty of this for you: no matter where you are on your success scale in life, you can change it right now if you want to. I should say, "If you choose to." If you are where you are in life right now based on the choices you've made, you can make a choice today to be in a different place in life tomorrow. Jim Rohn says, "You can't change your destination overnight, but you can change your direction overnight," again, with a choice to do so.

- What choices have you made that brought about negative results?

- What did you learn from that choice?

- What choice can you make today to create positive results?

- What choice do you want to make today that will put you in a different place in the future?

SUCCESS PRINCIPLES

There are hundreds of books on success along with the basic success principles. I've read many of these books and attended many trainings on the subject. I'm not pretending to be an expert, but I have personally applied these basic principles and have acquired a substantial amount of success in my life. So it is my desire to share my perspective and application of these principles with you. Here is a list of some of the principles we will be discussing and showing examples of their use. The main topic of this book is the first on this list, *belief*. In my experience, without belief, the other principles will only take you so far.

- Belief

- Vision

- Goal Setting/Planning

- Work Ethic

- Perseverance

- Personal Growth/Live Long Learning (Leaders are Readers)

- Affiliations/Building Relationships

- Well-Rounded Life (Body, Soul & Spirit)

- Communication/Listening Skills

- Excellence

- Humility

This book will discuss most of these principles through real life stories and application for how to take action on them and implement them into your life. The biggest emphasis of this book in the foundation of success is your belief. Remember, without a solid foundation you cannot build your house of success.

The main story I'm going to share with you is a true life story of success. This is not a Michael Jordan, Tiger Woods, Lance Armstrong, or Gandhi type of success story. This is a story about someone just like you. It's about a guy that believed in himself, utilizing this belief system, along with the basic success principles, to create that ultimate success. This success story is about someone I've known my entire life – myself! This story will take you through the ups and downs of my life experience. You will see how my belief and the choices I made along the way helped create my success.

Again, the main point I hope everyone gains from this is the power of belief. I want you to understand that belief is the foundation and starting point toward your success. I want you to realize that everyone including YOU can create ultimate success. To do this you must first believe in yourself, believe it is possible and believe you deserve it. The second thing is you must apply the other proven success principles to your plan and take action. Third, you have to stay the course. You cannot stop short and expect to reach your goals or vision. I don't golf, but I want to give you a visual example of this idea of stopping short: one hundred percent of every golf putt that is hit short of the hole will not go in. We need to putt it hard enough to go past the hole (set your goal high enough) to have a chance to go in (or achieve your goal). So don't quit. Don't stop short of what you desire or deserve.

As you read this story, understand it is not about the successes that were accomplished. It's about belief and use of success principles. It's about work ethic, ability to handle and overcome adversity, consistent vision and action taken toward plans over time. This story takes place with me starting out my life way below the standards of most

Americans – starting out financially, economically, and environmentally lower than most of you started out in life.

Success for everyone is different. Success is measured from where someone begins, where they have been, and where they end up in life. Every person's goals and dreams are different, so their measure of success is different. Never discount where someone is in life. It may be just what they dreamed about. Success in each person's view is different. The success you will read about here is what anyone and everyone can accomplish. Again, there are some attributes, principles, and mindset changes necessary to get there. You don't need to be average in life. You can be extraordinary. To accomplish your purpose or dream, you will need to make note of the thoughts, ideas and principles that are woven throughout my story as it weaves through the ups and downs of my life journey.

Before we start, I want to say again, that people really can accomplish their dreams in life. My wife and I have dreams together. Our dream is that we will have total financial and time freedom. We will have a place on the beach, and one in the deserts of Scottsdale, where our children still live. We will contribute to our church and charities, we will help our family, and we will help others accomplish this same place in life. We will have all these things because of the principles of life that we follow and the belief that we will get there. When we reach our goals, we will have all those things. Whatever your dreams are you can have them as well.

For those of you that are saying, "Here is another one of those books… that stuff never works!" The first lesson – for you – is, if that's what you think then you are right. With that mindset nothing will ever work for you anyway. For those of you that want to grow personally, have a better more positive mindset, better relationships, a better life, and you want to accomplish something great, read on!

CHAPTER TWO
MY STORY BEGINS

E ach and every one of us has a belief system because of where we were raised. The financial status we lived in was probably a big influence, whether positive or negative. The positive or negative surroundings of our families and friends is a big influence on most people. You may have lived in a household that was white collar, blue collar, rich, middle class, or poor. You may not have had much moral support, religious upbringing, or personal support. One belief I want to instill in all of you is that no matter your upbringing or support system, success is still possible for you.

I want to share with you how and where my mom and dad grew up. This will give you some insight into the long chain of poverty. This is a chain that can be broken by belief and success principles. My parents grew up in a very small town in South Eastern Tennessee named Charleston. Charleston is thirty miles north east of Chattanooga. The town had a population under 200 people and was basically a farming community. The main spot in town was the general store that doubled as the post office. This was a community where very few, if any people, had money. My mom, Betty, grew up as one of the poorest in the area. The following picture is of the home where my mom grew up. This was a two room shack which consisted of a kitchen and living area. She lived there with four other siblings, and her mother and father. There was no running water, they had an outhouse for a bathroom, and bathed in a tub where the water was heated up on the wood burning stove. In fact, all five kids would take turns bathing all in the same water. You can imagine how it would be if you were the last one in the tub.

All the children began working early in life. At a very young age, before and after school, they would all pick cotton, hoe weeds from the corn fields, weed the vegetable garden, and do many other jobs to help put food on the table. This created a very strong work ethic in my mom. All the kids had to take their lunch to school, which most times consisted of only a biscuit. My mom and family lived in dire poverty.

My dad didn't have much more, but did live on a family farm. He left school at an early age, after 8th grade. He used to say he taught the teachers everything he knew, then he left. At an early age he went off to join the Navy. This was his way of escaping the poverty in which he lived.

At age 21, John, my father, came back to Tennessee to visit family. While he was there, he went to a high school basketball game. That is when he saw Betty, his wife to be, and my mom. She was playing basketball for the high school team, even though she was only 13. John followed the school bus home to see where she lived. They met and he courted her. They weren't allowed to date alone so Betty's sister and brothers went with them to keep an eye on them. A year or so later, John moved Betty, her mom, Ruth, and 4 other brothers and a sister to San Diego where he was stationed in the Navy. John and Betty were married May 31st 1953; Betty was 14 years old. I know that 14 sounds pretty young, but she had good reason to get married at that age. One reason she married so young was to escape the poverty she lived through in Tennessee. She turned 15 the next day, June 1st. This was my parents' start in life together. They settled in National City, California not far from the naval base.

My story of success begins in National City, California, a suburb of San Diego. National City is in a triangle of three suburbs that would be considered the inner city or lower income area of San Diego (this area was similar to Watts in Los Angles). These three suburbs are Logan Heights, which is south east San Diego, The Barrio, which is underneath the San Diego Bay Bridge just south of San Diego, and National City. This is an area that had three different gang groups: Black gangs, Hispanic gangs, and Asian gangs. It was an area of drugs and violence, run down, broken down apartments and government housing. The area was littered with trash, filth and graffiti. The community was an area of high unemployment where people who were out of work were just hanging out, doing nothing to better their community. Because the streets were littered with filth, it had a musty, dirty smell to it. It was an area, where by age 21 a young man's life expectations were to have joined a gang, to have been shot, stabbed, killed or put in jail at some point. This was an area where the young people didn't have much hope of escape, much less success. Most young men in these types of areas see their only hope of escaping as becoming a professional athlete. I was no different. As I grew older, this also became a dream of mine as well.

I grew up in a small trailer park within this area. The trailer I grew up in was 8 feet wide by 35 feet long, *250 square feet* – not much bigger than a travel trailer. Most trailers in this park were very run down. It had a wash house and little area of dirt where we kids could play out of the streets. I lived in this trailer with my mother, father and brother. The income in the Navy was not very much. In the beginning, my mom was a stay-at-home mom. We lived on just a few hundred dollars a week, which at that time would have been considered poverty level.

My parents were very loving. My mother and father were supportive of almost everything I wanted to try. My father, even though he was supportive and loving, could also be very negative and was very prejudice against mixed marriages of blacks and whites. I was raised with a strong religious background and our family had very high moral standards. Both parents, because of their southern upbringing, stressed integrity and respect of others above all else. At age 17, my mom had her first child, and at age 18 she had her second child, me!

Since my father had only an 8th grade education, my mother went back to school after both children were born to get her GED. Even with their lack of education they always stressed the importance of getting a good education, having a strong work ethic, integrity, belief and a commitment to what you want. The most important belief they instilled in me was that I could be and have whatever I wanted in life.

As I grew up, my parents were both in the work force and my mother did several jobs, from being a secretary to selling AVON for extra money. She became an assistant pastor in her mid-20's and my father, after leaving the Navy, became a truck driver. To earn extra money, John, Betty, myself and my brother would collect cans, bottles, copper wire, and lead – basically anything that could be recycled into money. This was an excellent lesson for me and my brother. We learned to find ways to legally make extra money. This also taught us how to have a good work ethic, to do whatever it takes to put food on the table. Because of our religious background, I, along with my mother, brother and father, attended church on a regular basis; Sunday morning, Sunday afternoon rest-home service, Sunday night, Wednesday night and Friday night. That created a great belief system and moral background for me as a young man. This also kept both of us children out of trouble and spiritually grounded.

- Who taught you work ethic?

- Is your work ethic at a high enough level to create the success you want?

- Can you make a choice today, to do a little more each day so the compound effect creates your success?

Growing up, I never thought of myself as being poor, mainly because I didn't know any better. Everyone around me was in the same circumstances and I didn't see any differences. There were times, as I look back, I can remember how people looked at me as I walked by the low income, government housing projects. Occasionally, I would hear the kids calling me "trailer trash" and other harsh names. As we all know, kids can be cruel. But it didn't seem to bother me. I always had a positive outlook on life.

Every day I walked to school and passed gangs hanging out on street corners. Drugs were being sold. My brother and I had to find different ways to walk home from school to avoid the gangs and drugs. We never got involved in any of these activities. By the time my brother, Jim, was in middle school, he was beaten up several times by the gangs in the area. Most gang activity began in the middle school or teen years. The middle school had rival gang fights after school. These fights often included guns and switchblade knives. These fights often ended up with a few people getting stabbed.

Since the trailer we lived in was so small, Jim and I spent most of our spare time outdoors. We would play catch in the streets or on the dirt playground that was nearby our trailer. This is what I loved to do. Even at a very young age, I was very athletic. I could run really fast for my age. I also had excellent hand-eye coordination and could catch anything that was thrown my way.

Even though my parents didn't have much, they continually instilled in me the belief that I could do anything I wanted to, have anything I wanted to have, and be anything in life that I wanted to be.

Belief is the first principle you need to have in order to create success. Basically, it all starts in your mind with a single thought and a single belief that anything is possible. Most children grow up with their parents telling them that they can be an astronaut or president, whatever they wanted to be. But once people reach adulthood, they're told, "You can't do this and you can't do that. Are you crazy? That will never work."

I want to expand on this thought for a minute. Most people allow their belief system, their vision, their hope to fall apart because of this. In order to obtain and maintain your belief, you need to read positive personal growth materials and books. You need to surround yourself with people that have the same positive mindset that you have, and the same dreams of success. You need to stop listening to negative things like the news, or people around you that are telling you that you can't be or have what you want in life. If you think you can or you think you can't, you are right on both occasions. It is your thought process that helps your mind create plans and reach the goal you want to achieve. If you continue to believe you can do something, your mind will create a plan to achieve that goal. If you continue to think you can't do something, your mind will not work toward creating a plan for that goal; it will no longer try to reach it because you have basically already given up.

I want this book to help you regain your belief in yourself, to help you see that you can create the life you dreamed of. The accomplishments that I have achieved are not the focus of this book. It is simply my story showing that if I was able to create success, so can you. The accomplishments you read in this book are not to impress you, they are to impress upon you that you can have and do whatever you believe you can do. The focus is all about you and what you can accomplish. Now, back to my story....

In today's world, kids start playing organized sports at very young ages. Growing up, I never really got to play organized sports. The only way I played was in the streets or playgrounds near my trailer park, or during recess at school. Growing up, I always loved sports. I loved being outside running, playing catch, playing football, all the things most young boys like to do. At an early age I began watching sports on television, and started dreaming of one day playing football for a college, and then playing it professionally. Going pro was the dream of a lot of young people in neighborhoods like mine as it was a way to escape the poverty we lived in.

My parents always supported that dream, as they did with all of my dreams, telling me that I could do whatever I wanted to do. Even though I never played organized sports because of our financial situation, I continued to play in the streets almost every day, never giving up on my dream. When the kids played football, we used the street curbs as our out of bounds line, and cars as the touchdown line. I would come home with a lot of scrapes and bruises from falling on the hard pavement. I had a knack for the game of football, even at a young age. Whether it was a baseball, basketball or football, I could catch anything thrown my way. My hands were like glue. My dream progressed and became crystallized to one day be a football wide receiver. Even though I played all sports, my main focus was football. In fact, my dream was to play college football for the Texas Longhorns and for a coach named Darrel Royal.

In junior high, we moved from the bad neighborhood in National City to one that was still bad, but better than where we had been previously. The area was called Otay, which was south Chula Vista. We

ty for yourself and for where you are in life. Start hanging out with successful people. Stop hanging around those people that shoot you down. Start making choices that take you step-by-step closer to your goals and dreams. Start hanging out with your future, not your past.

- Who are you affiliating with?

- Can they help you reach your vision, goals or the level of success you desire?

- Do they discourage you and keep you down at their level?

- Make affiliations with those that encourage you and help you get where you want to go.

CHAPTER THREE
VISION OF SUCCESS

As many of you know, the type of area I lived in is usually described as a *ghetto*. As mentioned earlier, many young men dream of escaping the ghetto poverty, the gangs and the violence through athletics. Their dreams are to play college and then professional sports so that they can have a better life for themselves and their families. It is one of the only ways that they feel they have a chance to succeed. However, I was a little different. I had two plans. The first was to succeed in athletics and play professional football in order to have a better life. But, I was pretty realistic and also had a second plan, to get an education so that if the athletic career didn't work out, I could be a successful businessman. My parents, even though they didn't have much education, really stressed the importance of my education. They wouldn't allow me to play sports if the grades weren't there.

Through my middle school years, I began hanging out with the athletes in my school. We would plan to be at school early and play basketball or football. This helped me really begin to develop my athletic skills. By my 8th grade year, we were having very competitive games and this is where I began to flourish.

Where I went to middle school, the school included 7th, 8th and 9th grade. In my freshman year, it was the first year that I was able to participate in organized sports. The middle school had three sports I was able to participate in and I excelled in all three. I played football, basketball, and also ran track. In 9th grade, the school I went to only allowed freshman to play flag football. Even though this was not tackle football with pads, I was able to take my first step toward my dream of becoming a wide receiver. My team that freshman year went undefeated; as a wide receiver I was the top receiver on the team. I lead the team in touchdowns and receiving yards my freshman year. I actually ended up as one of the captains on the team.

In basketball, I had the same success. I was a starting forward on the team and I was one of the leading scorers and the leading rebounders. This was the year I really began to realize that I was blessed with exceptional physical skills, with speed and jumping ability. I ran track at the end of the year, mainly to stay in shape. My uncanny speed and leaping ability really helped me excel in sprinting and in the long jump. In fact, I was never beaten in a sprint or in the long jump that year. Because I excelled in all three sports, I was awarded the athlete of the year trophy for the school. This success increased my belief that my dream of professional sports was possible.

- Are you willing to spend extra time developing your skills?

- Are you willing to work a little more or a little harder each day to create your success?

- Will you put in the effort necessary to change your life?

The high school I attended was a three year high school; it included 10th, 11th and 12th grade. My first year of high school was my sophomore year. I went in with high expectations, both academically and athletically. This was going to be my first year of tackle football. I went into my sophomore year hoping to continue as a wide receiver. But when the coaching staff divided up the teams, the coaches put me on the defensive side of the football. I started the season as a free safety. I was very disappointed that I was not able to continue as a wide receiver; however, this didn't stop me from continuing the same work ethic and positive attitude that I had always had. I remained a free safety throughout the first eight games of the season. Even though this was not the position I wanted to play, I played it with everything I had. I didn't quit on my dream, even though this was a stumbling block.

As a safety, I was able to intercept the ball several times and was one of the leading tacklers on the team. I returned punts and kickoffs as well. Because I displayed an excellent work ethic and attitude, the coaches got together and gave me a chance to play wide receiver for the last four games of the season. The week prior to my first game as a wide receiver, I stayed after practice every day and worked extra on learning the plays, working with the quarter back on pass play timing, and preparing for that first game. I put the work ethic I had learned into practical application again. I spent hours every day that week learning plays and running routes.

The big day came when I was going to get my first shot as a wide receiver. This was the start of my dream coming true. I had an unbelievable game that day. I was able to catch four touchdown passes and had over 250 yards receiving. The next three games were duplicates. In only four games, I had caught more touchdowns and had more pass-catching yards than anyone else on the team. Because of this success, I was poised to go into my junior year with college scouts ready to look at me as a prospect. At this point in my life I felt like everything was going in the direction of my dreams.

Once football season ended, I went into basketball and had an excellent season. Basketball was still not a main focus for me. Even with that said, my sophomore year I was brought up to the varsity team to play the second half of the season. I was one of the leading rebounders and scorers on the team.

Track season came around and again I ran track. The events I ran were the 100, 200, four by 100 relay, long jump and the triple jump. I excelled in all of these events. In fact, I took first in almost every event I participated in. I made the varsity track team my sophomore year and was one of only two people to run on the varsity track team as a sophomore.

Spring football practice began in May of my sophomore year and I was very excited to get back out on the field. During spring practice, they were running plays without pads, testing the athletes for speed, agility, quickness and other drills. Spring training was used to place players for the following season in the correct positions. I really excelled at the spring training. My stats were already at college and professional levels. I ran the forty yard dash on grass with football cleats with a 4.3 second time. In 1972 that time was considered world-class speed. I was the fastest on the team. My vertical jump was 42 inches, which was uncanny for my age. With these two accomplishments, and the ability to catch anything I touched, I was poised for college talent scouts to start recruiting me after my junior year. Life was going along just as planned, actually even better than imagined. I was on top of the world and saw my dreams getting closer.

During the summer between my sophomore and junior year, the basketball team participated in summer league basketball. This was a great way for me to stay in shape and improve my skills as a basketball player. I was doing well as a starter with the varsity team. I was again a leading rebounder and scorer as the summer progressed. Just prior to the last game of summer league, the team was going through their normal warm-up routine. I felt some pain in my upper back and was talking to a teammate about the pain. My friend Eric said, "Let me crack your back. I think your back is just out of place." So Eric picked me up from behind with his arms across my chest and as he squeezed me, I heard a cracking noise. I felt a sharp pain in my neck. Even with the pain, I continued with my pre-game warm-ups and started the game. It hurt me just to run up and down the court. There was even a sharp pain when I breathed in deeply. But my adrenalin was so strong that I played the whole game. In fact, it was one of my best games of the summer league. I scored 18 points and had 11 rebounds.

Once the game was over and the excitement and adrenalin left me, I collapsed from the intense pain in my neck and back. I was taken to the hospital immediately after the game. I had X-rays and MRIs taken of my neck and back. My parents were very concerned about what was going on. I spent the night in the hospital waiting for the doctor to come in. The next day, my doctor came in to give me and my parents the results of what he had found. The noise I had heard when my buddy cracked my back was a fracture of my 7th vertebrate in my neck. I had basically broken my neck! The doctor also found that I had a condition in my lower back similar to a slipped disc. The slipped disc was something that I had from birth.

The doctor continued with the news of what this meant. He told me and my parents that I would never play football again. This was a devastating blow for me and I cried for quite a while that day. My number one dream, my hope for a better life, my vision was over in a fraction of a second.

It's not what happens to you in life, it's how you handle what happens to you.

- What adversity have you been faced with in your life?

- What did you learn from it?

- How did you react to it?

- Did you quit and say this is not to be or did you change your direction and still create success?

Most people would have allowed this event to derail them in life. Some people would have used this as an excuse to not continue striving for success. But, as I've said earlier, if you want to have what most people will never have, you have to believe and do the things most people aren't willing to do. This belief in success was instilled in me. As I recovered in the hospital, I began to stop feeling sorry for myself and formulated my plan B. I would continue studying harder than ever for the chance to be successful someday in business. But, I also turned my athletic focus to basketball. Statistically, it was harder to get a basketball scholarship than a football scholarship. Only 3.4% of high school basketball players get a NCAA scholarship and 6.5% of football players get one. I was starting my focus on basketball pretty late in the game. My junior year was coming up, which is when college scouts are looking for players.

My parents had no extra money for any basketball equipment like a backboard and rim. My father, however, worked for a lumber and gravel company at the time and was able to get a wooden pole about 14' long and a piece of plywood that he cut in the shape of a basketball backboard. He erected this on the dirt playground next door to our trailer so when I came home from the hospital I would be able to practice as much as I wanted. Again, the work ethic came into play. I shot, dribbled, and practiced the fundamentals every day. I would do this for hours. In fact, I took thousands of shots and dribbled the ball everywhere I went. When school started I would play 3-5 hours after my homework was completed. On Saturday and Sunday I was playing at the gym from when it opened at 12 until it closed at 6. Part of my daily routine, when I was ready to stop for the day, was that I would take 100 more shots. My goal was to make 70% of them or I couldn't stop. I would also never leave the court on a missed shot. This was all part of the mindset necessary for me to have success. I never wanted to quit on a missed shot or a poor performance. By doing this, I ended with success and it created positive momentum for the next day. My actions were working hard toward excellence.

Perfecting the fundamentals in a sport or a job is aspiring for excellence in what you do. To have more success, never stop on an unsuccessful sales call. Make another call until you have success so that you have that momentum of success to build on the next day. My routine went on for the next three months until basketball season started. When basketball season arrived and practice started, I was ready. During practice, on every wind sprint, running stairs, or any drill, I gave 100% and was 1st to finish almost every time. This was the continuation of my belief and work ethic. I was ready for the season!

- Perfect the fundamentals.

- Perfect the process.

- Take action immediately.

- Create your own success.

When the basketball season started, the team was made up of two sophomores, two juniors and one senior. We were one of the least experienced teams in the area. This was also one of the smallest high schools in the San Diego area with only eleven hundred students. Despite being an underdog, our team did well, winning eighteen of our twenty-eight games. Because of my work ethic and commitment during my off-season regiment, I excelled. I was recognized my junior year as one of the top players in the area. I was selected to be featured in the magazine *Prep Athletes* as one of the top 25 prep athletes to watch going into their senior year. My goal of playing athletics in college and possibly as a professional was still there.

During my senior year, our team won twenty-eight games and lost only five. Even the losses were close. One loss was in double overtime, one in triple overtime and one was a last second shot. My team won our conference. We went on to the San Diego County Championships. The final games were to be played in the San Diego sports arena where there would be a lot of college scouts. In these championships, we competed with schools that had four and five thousand students. Even though we were considered highly under-dogged, we took third in the San Diego County Championships. I made the San Diego County All-Star team and played an exhibition game in the summer for college scouts. I was extremely excited with the news that I had several scholarship offers at the end of my senior year. This meant that I was in the top 96% of all high school basketball players in the U.S. This was great because my parents were unable to financially send me to college.

Even though I was now focused on basketball, I still concentrated on my education. I wanted to be prepared for success in business if my athletic career ended in college. I had scholarship offers to play at the Naval Academy, Pepperdine, United States International University, Idaho State, Weber State, San Diego State, UC Riverside and others. I chose a small school in Northern California, California State University, Chico. This school was only a NCAA division II college, but had a great schedule. In the pre-season they played against USF when Bill Cartwright (future Chicago Bulls center) was there, and Santa Clara when Kurt Rambis (of the LA Lakers) was there.

We did not, however, do well against these elite schools. My college team was only average. On a personal note I did well, but never was able to excel as I did in football. In the end of my college playing days, I did not go any further into an athletic career. My dream of professional athletics as an escape was over. But I did not let this get me down! I finished college and received my Bachelor's degree with a 3.2 GPA.

Remember earlier when I said that everyone has ups and downs in life? Everyone has disappointments. How you handle them makes all the difference. Every successful person remains focused on their goal. They remain focused on their dreams. Nothing stops them from staying committed to their vision. Their persistence and consistent effort over time is what separates success and failure. One factor in overcoming disappointments is to be grateful for what you have. There are always people that have less than you do. They have more difficulty than you do. If you keep your focus on what your dream is, stay positive, continue to take one step at a time toward your dream, you will have it.

CHAPTER FOUR
PURSUING PLAN B

With my athletic career behind me and a business career in front of me, I was off to a new chapter in my life where I would be able to put my success attributes into play. I still had great belief based on my childhood and my successes along the way. I knew I would have great success in anything I did. I started pursuing that plan B business career.

I landed my first job within a month of looking as a management trainee at a finance company. I only worked in that career for six months, realizing that I could not use my full potential in that job. I was looking for something where I could use my personal people skills coaching and natural sales ability. In February of 1981, I landed a job with the largest consumer products company in the world. This was a great training ground for me and it helped me grow personally because of the training that the company supplied. I took the same work ethic, the same belief, the same commitment into this job. I strived for excellence using the same self-confidence that I used in my athletic career into the business career and quickly excelled within the company. I received my first promotion after a year and half in the company and I was promoted several times within my fifteen year career.

My belief, and use of the other success principles, was bringing me the same success levels in business that it did in athletics. In the late 1980's there were some economic downturns and my company reorganized three times. Even with the reorganizations, I continued to be promoted. At this point, I felt it was necessary to further my education. This education would help me go further in either the corporate world or as entrepreneur. Remember, my parents stressed education even though they only had and 8th grade and GED education. So I entered the MBA program at the University of Phoenix in 1990 and completed my degree in 1992. I finished with a 3.66 GPA. I completed my graduate program while working full time at the consumer products company, and also with having a two-year-old son and a newborn daughter.

- Are you too busy to improve yourself?

- Are you too busy to create the success you deserve and desire?

- Are we making excuses on why you can't reach your dream?

- We can either make excuses or create success, we can't do both!

I share these factors of having kids and working full-time because I believe they are important for you to know. We all think we are busy in life and that we are not able to accomplish our dreams and goals. I was very busy, but became very focused on the success I envisioned to provide for my family. By completing my graduate degree, I was one step closer to the success I believed I deserved.

In February of 1996, after fifteen years, the consumer products company was reorganizing once again. They were offering severance packages for higher paid executives to leave the company on a voluntary basis. I took this as another opportunity to grow my success somewhere else and accepted one of those packages. I already had a job lined up before I left. In my next venture I was hired as the chief operating officer (COO) of a national sales and camping company. This was very exciting for me because I had reached another top pinnacle of success. Being hired as a C-level executive is the top rung in the corporate success ladder. Only the top one tenth of one percent ever make it to this level. So again, my belief, my work ethic, my preparation to have success all helped carry me to that next pinnacle of success in my life.

After five years of running this company, economic times affected the bottom line of the company and I helped the owners wind down the company; by 2001 they went out of business. This left me with another challenge. I wondered, *where do I go from here?* It was an economy where jobs were scarce. Then my wife, Donna, approached me with an idea of going into the mortgage industry. She was always very supportive of my skills and attributes, and believed strongly in my capabilities to have success in whatever I did. She was in the mortgage industry on the mortgage insurance side. She knew all the top players in the area and made introductions to the owners or leaders where she felt there was the best opportunity and the most integrity. On my first interview I was hired as a loan originator with a mortgage company.

In June of 2001, I began the next chapter in my business career. My belief was still strong that I could have success in anything, and I worked hard to learn this new industry. I also had great mentors to help show me the ropes. It's always important to surround yourself with the most successful people to help you create your own success. Two gentlemen, named Fred Kron and Erik Lutz (co-owners of the company) helped guide me in this new industry. I quickly had great success within this new industry. After a year and a half in this business I was making more money than when I was a COO. I continued through this career from 2001 until 2008.

In 2007, the real estate market and the economy nationally crashed. In January of 2008, I lost 90% of my income. I was affected by the crash more than most. My loan pipe line in the mortgage industry consisted mainly of jumbo loans and investment construction loans. This was approximately 90% of my portfolio. In January of 2008, the federal government eliminated those programs, which means that I lost most of my income. At this point, I was devastated, based on the fact that I and my wife, Donna, had four children all nearing the college age or already in college. Even though my income was gone, we were still grateful that Donna had her corporate job.

Donna's income was over half of our total income. As most of you know, most families live life close to what they make as a household. Even with this set-back financially, my glass was always half full. At this point in my life I was now in my 50's, overqualified, over educated and had made too much money to be able to find a job in a devastated economy. I could not even get responses to my resume submissions for lower-level management positions. When I did, the hiring company would simply say, "We cannot afford someone like you." Even though I was willing to take less income, the companies still felt that I would leave as soon as something better came along.

So the corporate world at this point did not seem like an option for me. My family and I were praying for an opportunity to show up on the horizon so that we could continue to prosper and grow financially. In April of 2008, a good friend invited me and Donna to take a look at a business that had residual income, up front bonuses, and sounded recession proof. So we agreed to meet on a Monday for lunch to hear about this new business opportunity. When we arrived, our friend introduced us to a lady named Mindy Deeble. Mindy was introduced as a top executive in the company and she explained the details of the business. As she went through the business plan, the business just made sense. To be paid on your own expenses, that you had to pay anyway, expenses like cell phones, gas, electricity, credit card processing, television service, internet service, with all the main carriers. The business helped customers save money on their expenses and I would still be able to make money on my customers' services. The company also paid upfront bonuses to bring in customers and other business owners for the company.

As Donna and I left the meeting and walked outside, we looked at each other and said, "This would work." We had never been involved in a direct marketing company (MLM) before, but felt that with the mentorship and trainings that were available, we could have success. At this point, I did not have many choices. So we met with Mindy Deeble and got started in the business on April 15th of 2008. I got into action immediately and applied the same success principles that had created success in every aspect of my life. I began again, with the belief that I could and would have success in this business as well.

Within a week I had hit the first paying position in the company called Executive Team Trainer. Within three and half weeks, I hit the second position in the company called Executive Team Leader. Along the way in my first month, I was able to max out the bonus structure from the first position and made $3,000. Even though this was not the money I was used to making, I knew this was just the start. Donna and I, together (Donna working part-time along with her full-time job), worked the business and worked extremely hard to create success for others who had joined our organization. Within six months, I had hit a third position called Team Coordinator and had even helped someone who lived in Tucson, Arizona hit that position two weeks later.

This was a business that fit everything I was looking for in my life. The ability to not just help myself, but to be able to help hundreds and someday tens-of-thousands of people improve their lives financially, personally, spiritually and emotionally. This was a dream come true. Donna and I continued to work hard at the business, applying all the attributes necessary for success. We had great belief, a strong work ethic, were committed, persistent, and very coachable. By our 15th month, we hit a top position in the company called 3 Star Regional Vice President. Things were going along toward our personal and financial dreams better than planned.

In February of 2010, my wife was called into a meeting with her boss. The company was in financial trouble and was looking for any reason to downsize and eliminate the higher-paid employees. She was one of the fatalities of this downsizing. Even though we were doing well in our current company, we had another huge financial nut to crack. We had a 5,000 square foot home in a prominent area. All four children were in college and we were paying the tuition. So we really needed the income and insurance that my wife's company provided.

This job loss really affected my wife mentally and then started to affect me as well. We became fearful and desperate in our daily activities in our MLM business. We began to lose that belief that we had had our whole lives. This spiral took us to a place where we were almost ready to give up on our business and our dreams.

Then we both started seeking mentoring and support from personal growth books, CD's and individuals that were having success in their business. We even contacted the president of our current business and he agreed to support and mentor us. In our 1st conversation with the company president, Mr. Greg Provenzano, he asked some tough questions that caused us to do some self-reflection. In times of adversity, even the strongest people can falter in their beliefs. This was where I was when this self-reflection occurred; we were at the lowest point in our business. In fact, we produced more in our 1st week in the business than we did during this particular month.

We both looked ourselves in the mirror and honestly assessed where we were and what we needed to do. I began doing the things that got me to the level of success that I started with in this company, and what created my success in everything I had ever done in life. I renewed my belief through my spiritual side primarily. I began to be grateful for what I had. I began to focus on my dreams and believed they were already manifested in my life, all because of the principle we are discussing in this book.

- Do you see yourself living the life you dream of?

- Do you write down your goals and create a plan to create your dreams?

- Will you do whatever it takes to create your dream?

It all starts and ends with you, belief in yourself. Not only that you can accomplish your goals, but that you *will* accomplish them. You need a clear vision of what you see as success and then create a plan to accomplish that goal. You need to let others close to you know what your goals are. This puts your goals out there in the public so that those people you confide in will hold you accountable for them. You have to remain consistent and persistent over a long period of time. Your work ethic has to be stronger than anyone else. You have to be willing to do those things that others are not willing to do.

Our president, Greg Provenzano, has said, "If you are too big to do the small things, then you are too small to receive the big things in life." Always be humble and put other's interests before your own. There have been a lot of great leaders in this world. One of them was a really great general named Napoleon. He always helped his men get their goals accomplished first. This created great success for him along with the undying loyalty of his men. Remember, we never get to the top of anything alone. It takes a team.

I want to summarize my story and successes in my life. In my current MLM business, I have really been blessed and I get to train, coach and mentor thousands of people from a stage. When people see me on stage with a custom suit, hopefully sounding polished, they don't know where I came from and the struggles I had to go through to create my success in life.

My hope by writing this book, I can bring hope to those of you out there that have no hope. If I can grow up in the ghettos and succeed in life, then so can you. I hope that you can see by the struggles I endured that success is on the other side of those failures and struggles. Don't turn back. Keep moving forward. Keep believing in yourself. Keep focused on those dreams. Keep applying the principles you learned in this book, and others that you need to learn. Keep personally growing so that you can have more and more success. Keep helping pull others along with you on this journey called life. It's a lot more fun to have success by helping others have theirs.

- Are you thinking only of yourself and your success?

- Are you helping others create their success?

- Are you thinking outside the norm to get where you want to go? If you keep doing what you're doing, you will only have what you already have.

I want to share a thought with all of you. The thought is that if you believe in yourself, if you create a clear vision and set goals, if you create a plan to achieve those goals and dreams, you can and will achieve them. My parents' lives and my own life are a great example of what can be accomplished. I want to share with all of you where my parents are today in life. My parents still live in a trailer. They have upgraded to a double-wide and they own the space they live on. That trailer park has barbed wire on the top of the fence so it's still not the best area, but it's where they want to live. It is one block from their church. My mom, Betty, is still a pastor at the Country Church in Chula Vista California. They have never made much money. The most they have ever made is about $15,000, maybe $18,000 in a year. My father, John, after driving a truck for 22 years was medically retired with a bad lower back. So they lived on a very minimal retirement, social security and a pastor's salary.

With that said, my mom and dad over time kept collecting bottles, cans and other recyclables to earn additional money. My mom used that additional $25 dollars or $50 per month, to pay for small home building lots, in the mountains outside of San Diego. She would trade a small lot for a bigger lot and then pay that one off. They started building homes on these lots. They would then sell the home and would hold the paper on the loan and have the buyer pay them the interest to buy instead of the bank. Today they are probably worth $500,000 to $750,000 in real estate, cash, IRA's and savings accounts and never made more than a few hundred dollars a week (while the average American has only about $30,000 saved toward retirement). Their goal of success was to be able to take care of themselves, but also to leave money to their children. They have obviously accomplished that. This is a willingness to do whatever it takes to make their dreams and goals come true.

Do those things that others won't do, like pick up cans. I remember when I was in college my mom dad and brother would collect and recycle cans and bottles just so they could send me an extra $20 bucks a month to have a little money to spend. I am so grateful to my parents for instilling in me a spiritual foundation, a belief system that I could and would do anything in life I wanted, a work ethic, a do whatever it takes attitude. They taught me humility, that I was not better than anyone else, I was not above doing anything necessary to accomplish my dreams. One of the most important things I learned was to be a servant to others, love others no matter what. Always put others before myself. All these things have helped me have success in life and they can help you do the same.

- What are you willing to do to create a better life for you and your family?

- Are you willing to be humble and do things others aren't willing to do?

- Are you willing to take the extra effort necessary to get where you want to go?

CHAPTER FIVE
BELIEF, CHOICES AND PERSEVERANCE

I t doesn't matter what business you are in. It doesn't matter what your vision of success is. It doesn't matter where you start in life with belief and application of these success principles. I know for a fact that every one of you can reach your ultimate success.

Here is a brief story of someone that started his life from a much better place in life. I have some good friends named Todd & Erica Stottlemyre. Todd played baseball in the major leagues. Todd's father, Mel, was a pitcher for the New York Yankees at a time when they had some of the greatest players ever to play baseball. He was also, for many years, the pitching coach for the New York Yankees. Todd's playground growing up was Yankee Stadium. He was able to be around people like Whitey Ford, Mickey Mantle, Roger Maris, his father Mel, and many other great baseball players.

Todd, through his belief in himself, choices he made along the way and his application of these same success principles, played fifteen years as a major league baseball player. As a pitcher, Todd was on three World Series Championship teams. He won two back-to-back titles with Toronto and one with the Arizona Diamond Backs.

Even with his successes, Todd had to overcome many struggles along the way. He had the baggage of living up to his father, Mel's, success as a professional baseball player. People would say, "You aren't as good as your father." He told me about a time early in his career when he was struggling with his pitches. He was dropped down to the minor leagues. This was a devastating blow to Todd. He is a very proud, persistent, consistent, and hard-working guy. He had to develop a few other pitches to be successful in the major leagues. When he went down to the minors, he listened to the coaches; he worked hard and was able to develop other pitches. Most importantly, he made the decision that he would never go down to the minors again.

Based on his belief, vision, work ethic, and perseverance (no quit attitude) he stayed in the major leagues for the rest of his career. The rest is history for Todd and his accomplishments in baseball and in his business career. He went on to be successful in several other businesses after baseball.

I share this clip of Todd's story with you because I want you to understand that it doesn't matter where you start in life. It matters how and where you finish. You can have everything you deserve by applying these same principles, whether you're poor and from a ghetto like me, or you came from money. Success is available for everyone that is willing to work hard enough, long enough and smart enough.

- Do you have the necessary desire to reach your goals?

- Do you have the commitment level necessary to reach your goals?

- Do you have the persistence (no quit, do whatever it takes attitude) to reach your goals?

Here is another success story of a friend of mine, John Lang. John was from a totally different industry than Todd. John is from the real estate and development business world. I have known John and his wife Diane going on eight years now. John is one of the most successful people I know.

When John and I started talking about how he created his success, he began telling me something his grandfather said. He told John, "The only thing you have in life is your reputation." John has lived his life by that.

John grew up in East Meadows, New York. John grew up in what he describes as a lower middle class household. His father made about $400 per month gross and they lived in a 1,000 square foot home.

Growing up, John's father, Robert W. Lang, and other mentors, like his teachers and coaches, gave him solid principles verbally and by examples that helped him create his success in life. The same principles we have discussed throughout this book, belief, perseverance, work ethic and others. When I asked John what helped him the most to create his success, he said his belief that he could do anything and his perseverance (no quit attitude). John told me that he was good at a lot of things but he wasn't the best. He became successful by surrounding himself with people that had strengths he didn't have.

John had success in athletics at an early age. He was part of a State Championship Little League baseball team. Then John attended a private Lutheran School where his teachers and coach continued to mentor him in these principles. In high school he was part of a National Championship basketball team. He went on to Roanoke

College in Virginia where he was part of a College NCAA II National Championship team. He realized from these team sports that you need to surround yourself with good players (or people) to create the ultimate success.

He took that same attitude into the business world. Once he graduated from college he began a career in real estate. John mentioned his plan to someone at church and they told him that they heard the test was tough and only one out of three people pass it. John's response was that he felt sorry for the two people sitting on either side of him during the test. This showed his belief in himself. John passed the test, but struggled for six or eight months before he got the business going.

By applying the principles we are discussing, he started having success in real estate. He was offered an opportunity to move to Boca Raton, Florida to start another real estate company. John jumped at the opportunity and became even more successful in Florida. He expanded his real estate company to include property management and sales and marketing of homes for builders. As time passed, John gained a property management client in Scottsdale, Arizona and began to spend a lot of time in Arizona. John's partner approached him saying he was spending so much time in Arizona, maybe he should move there. The partner offered to buy the Florida company and its assets. John agreed and he moved to Scottsdale and went to work for Dixon Group PLC.

This is where the massive success began for John. He then started a company called Pinnacle Development. He surrounded himself with people that had strengths he didn't have and they started. John worked in his basement for four years without a paycheck to get a project called Estancia off the ground. Estancia is a very high end home development in Scottsdale. The homes are 10,000 square feet and larger with price tags in the millions of dollars. During the four years of toiling in his basement, he was contacted daily by people saying he couldn't do what he was proposing to do with Estancia. He had people trying to buy it from him. John and his team continued to work and believe in the vision of the project. When they launched the project to sale, it became one of the most successful home development projects in Arizona history.

John and his team went on to develop many more projects like Seven Canyons in Sedona, projects in Hawaii, California, Austria, and Texas to name a few. At one point, John and his partners owned thousands of acres of land appraised at $400,000,000 and the debt was only $120,000,000. I share this because this shows John's massive success in the development world. With John's success he was able to surround himself with some of the top business and financial leaders in the United States. In John's success, he had a lot of choices to make to get to his vision of success. If he did not believe in himself and if he wouldn't have persevered toward his goal, he would not have had huge success.

John gave me a great quote of his, "Life is nothing but a series of choices and the choices you make define who you are and who you become". I asked John if he would sum up how he created success. He said, "Believe in yourself and what you are doing. Always have integrity, and perseverance, never quitting on your dreams."

- Are you making choices to move forward toward success?

- Are you making choices to grow personally to be prepared for success?

- Are you surrounding yourself with the right people that will help you create success?

TAKING RESPONSIBILITY

At this point I want to remind you of some thoughts that I started this book with. In order for you to create success, it is critical that you take responsibility for where you are in life. We are right where we are supposed to be based on the choices that we have made in our lives. We made those choices based on the influences that we allowed to become our moral compass in life. We all had people who came into our lives and taught us what they believed to be true and right or wrong. They set examples for us based on how they lived their lives. We had the choice to take from these influences what we wanted to incorporate into our lives. Here are some quick examples of what I'm talking about: I've heard a lot of sob stories about how some people had a parent who was an alcoholic and so they became an alcoholic themselves. I've also heard people that came from poor backgrounds, like I did, say that they didn't have a chance in life because of where they came from. These are all choices that each individual believed, so that is what happened in their lives.

I want to share a few examples of people that faced issues, but made choices to have a better life. They believed they deserved more, so they made choices to be different than what they experienced in life. My wife, Donna, had a mother growing up who was an alcoholic and misused prescription drugs. Her mother was also married seven times before the age of 40. When Donna was about seven and her sister Debbie was around five, their mother married a man named Jimmy White. He was a very stable part of their lives. Jimmy instilled in them a work ethic and the importance of education. They choose to follow his example in life and even though Jimmy and their mom divorced after a few years, they still stay in touch with Jimmy today.

Donna's mom never really made much money in her life. In fact, they would have been considered at the poverty level financially. This created a very unstable home environment for Donna and her sister Debbie. Both Donna and Debbie made a different choice for their lives and families. They both became very successful. Debbie is a nurse in her hometown in Mississippi. Her husband Russell is a nurse anesthesiologist with a master's degree in the subject. They do not drink and have a very stable marriage with two adult children, McGuire and Russel.

Donna has been very successful in her careers, financially, and in her marriage to me. Donna has been in the top 5% of money earners in the United States for 16 years. These ladies made the choice not to be like their mother. They believed that there was something better in their future than they had experienced in their past. They made a choice to have a better life personally and financially, created a plan and took action on that plan.

I have a friend from the gym where I work out by the name of Corey Yasuto Gaines. Corey is of African American/Japanese descent and was raised in Lynwood/Compton, California in an area called Nickerson Gardens (this area was the projects). Corey's parents were both raised and went to high school at Jordan High School in an area called Watts. The Watts and Compton areas are underprivileged areas in Los Angeles, very similar to where I grew up.

When Corey was young, his father, Winslow Gaines, spent quality time with him. Corey's father was a great role model and taught him belief in himself, work ethic, integrity, and many other great qualities. Corey's father told him a lot of great things to help him through adversity and to help him create success. One of his father's sayings was "It only takes one person to believe in you, and that's you." He also told Corey, "If you don't believe in yourself, how can you expect others to believe in you?" These thoughts are foundational for not just Corey's success, but for yours.

When Corey was in middle school, they were bussing kids from his neighborhood to an all-white school. Corey was bused to a middle school in Westwood, California called Emerson in a very affluent area of Los Angeles. Corey had choices to make in this situation. He could have had a chip on his shoulders or he could make the most of this as an opportunity. Corey used this as an opportunity, and he had a chance to see what was possible in life with success.

I'm sure at first this was uncomfortable for him, but he made the choice to make the most of the opportunity. Based on his belief in himself, and his work ethic, he became a McDonald's All American in high school, and attended UCLA on a basketball scholarship. He was drafted into the NBA and played there for five years with Seattle, Philadelphia, Denver, New Jersey, and the New York Nicks. Corey then played in Europe for almost fifteen years in places like Italy, Turkey, Greece, Russia, Japan and his last five years in Israel. Corey then became the head coach of the Phoenix Mercury and had success there. He is currently an assistant coach with the Phoenix Suns in charge of the offense.

Corey did have his ups and downs, as we all do. It is how he handled it and what he learned from it that continued his success (like all successful people do). According to Corey, his success came from his belief in himself and his vision of a better life. With the role model of his father and his perseverance (no quit attitude) he made great choices along the way to get there.

- Do you believe in yourself?

- Do you believe you can and will accomplish your goals and dreams?

- Will you do whatever it takes to get there?

The last story I want to share with you about choices, is to me the most impactful. I've had many mentors in my life, personally and professionally. This story is about two of my mentors and now very close friends from the network marketing business I started in 2008. My mentors were Jeremy and Mindy Deeble. Two of the nicest, most humble, and hardest working people I've ever known. I've always believed one key to having success is about who you surround yourself with. You need to surround yourself with people that are successful and have what you want. Jeremy and Mindy are two of those people.

Mindy and Jeremy grew up in what they describe as lower middle class. Mindy's father was a Wonder Bread salesman and worked for the company for 27 plus years. Mindy got a lot of her work ethic from his example and also from how hard her mom worked at home. Mindy had 6 other siblings and this family of 9 lived in a very small home with 3 bedrooms and 1 bath until her sophomore year of high school. Jeremy lived very similarly. His father had a paper route, which Jeremy helped his father with, and other odd jobs.

Starting at a very young age, both Mindy and Jeremy had to work for everything they wanted in life. Nothing was ever just given to them. Both Mindy and Jeremy feel grateful for growing up this way. It helped create a desire to have more, a work ethic and the perseverance to create their future success. Because of how she grew up, Mindy at the young age of 12, came to the realization that there had to be a better way to live. Now I know what you must be thinking, that this is uncanny; most people think where they are in life is just the way it is and how it will always be. Mindy just refused to believe her life had to always be like this! She had a huge desire to make something big happen so that she never had to be in that situation again.

Jeremy and Mindy finished high school and went into the work force. They both figured that if they just worked really hard then they could eventually have more. Mindy worked 4 different jobs right out of high school. She worked as a cookie lady (selling cookies to businesses) in the mornings, retail stores (selling clothing) in the afternoons & evenings, and on weekends taking the graveyard shifts at Hewlett Packard testing disks. Jeremy worked several jobs as well, working as many hours as he possibly could. When they were 19 and 20 years old, Jeremy and Mindy were married.

In the very beginning of their marriage, they started in a network marketing company hoping that they could create the life they truly wanted. However, by the time Mindy was 26 they already had 4 children and life hit them in the face. Jeremy was doing whatever he could to put food on the table and pay the bills. Mindy ran a childcare out of their home so she could stay home with the children. They have told me that there were many times that they didn't have the money to buy all the groceries they needed.

So this was a tough time for them. However, because they had joined this network marketing company and were able to be around people who wanted more, they started to think and carry themselves differently than how they had learned growing up. You see, they learned a huge key to success and that is that if you want something more, then you need to become more (personal growth). That is exactly what they did.

During those five years, they did a lot of personal growth by reading, listening to trainings in their car and going to training events that helped them think bigger. They worked hard for five years, but never made any money. However, failure can't cope with persistence. As they continued to work on themselves, their life started getting better. They never made any money from that first network marketing company, however, things started to improve in their life because they continued to work on themselves.

Jeremy eventually started working at the Statesman Newspaper to pay the bills. This job at least gave them a little bit more stability, however it made Jeremy work a lot of hours and work on Sunday's, which completely went against their beliefs. Jeremy and Mindy are very strong in their spiritual beliefs and wanted to attend church on Sundays as a family. So they made a decision for Jeremy to quit and find other work. Mindy told me at this point that they believe that if you do the right thing, good things will happen for you. She was right! A month later, a friend of Jeremy's called and said his father-in-law was looking for someone to help him in his grocery store cart care business. Jeremy started to work for him and did very well. His boss became his mentor in business and taught him a lot about success.

Jeremy eventually bought the business from his boss and this was a big turning point in his business career. They did very well financially. In fact they paid off the debt from buying this company and owned it free and clear. Even though they were finally able to build their home that they had always dreamed of, they believed there was more in life for them personally and financially. After eight years in the cart care business, Jeremy and Mindy were introduced to another network marketing company. In a matter of six months of joining the company, they tripled their income and were able to walk away from the cart care business. Nine months later, they hit a top position in the company that literally changed their life financially. After just three and a half years in this business, they hit the top position of the company called Senior Vice President. At this position in the company they have made millions.

Jeremy and Mindy have been in the top 100 money earners of all network marketing companies in the world for as long as I have known them. That makes them a top 1% money earners here in the United States. They owe all this to their belief that they deserved more in life, and that they could and would have success because of their work ethic, perseverance and commitment. They had a lot of choices to make along the way to get to the top. At one point early in their business, their family made fun of them and ridiculed them about choosing to pursue this business. Mindy's father would make her cry when he teased her about this choice. Jeremy and Mindy held strong in their belief that it would work and chose to stick it out. It obviously paid off for them. In fact during the 2008 economy down turn, Mindy's father lost all of his retirement in real estate investments. Jeremy and Mindy were able to put her parents on their payroll and they will never have to worry about money again. It was totally all about their belief and their choices in life.

These five stories are about people from different economic and business pursuits, yet all of them found success using the same principles.

- How do you react to the opinions of others?

- Do you maintain your focus on your vision, goals and dreams?

- Do you allow others opinions to dictate your success?

We as individuals have the *choice* to learn from others and take from them what we want to emulate in order to create our own lives. Based on our belief in ourselves and our vision, the application of the success principles discussed in this book and the action we take on the written plan is critical to create our success. By creating the plan and taking action on the plan, we will live the life we want and deserve.

At the beginning of this book I shared some information about my parents. They were really great parents. They both had a lot to offer that helped me create my life plan. The biggest thing they both gave me was belief in myself that I could be and do anything in life that I wanted to. There were also some things I choose not to take with me on my journey. My father, for instance taught me work ethic, right from wrong, integrity, and many other great things. In fact, my favorite saying from my dad that he would say to me and I still use today is, "Luck is where opportunity and preparation meet". This was from a man with very little education, but a lot of street smarts. However my father was not perfect; things I did not take from him were how he treated my mother and his negative view of life. He was very condescending and at times not verbally kind to mom. He suffered from depression. He was also very prejudice against African-Americans. In fact my daughter, Amber, recently married a very nice young man named Tyler McClendon. Tyler's father is black and his mother is white. My father, choose not to attend the wedding and said that if she married Tyler he would disown her. My father's behavior and attitude broke my heart and Amber's heart. But I made a choice growing up that I would not judge by color, I would see the person. I made a choice to be positive like my mother. I made a choice of how I would be and how I would raise our children.

I have listed the success principles below again that I shared in the beginning of this book. I want to explain each one, what my theory on it is, and how you can apply it to your life. If you really want more from life, if you really want a better life, if you really believe you deserve more and if you are willing to do what it takes to create your success, applying these principles will help you achieve it.

CHAPTER SIX
THE PRINCIPLES

BELIEF

S o now let's talk about belief. It is my perspective and my research of successful people that proves that the foundation of success is belief. Without belief in yourself, belief that you deserve more in life, belief in your vision of success, belief in the plan to accomplish your vision, there can be no success. Without belief, the other success principles can only take you so far. Plus, you will not be able to sustain that success. It is through my research of successful people and my firm belief that anyone can create and have whatever level of success they **believe** they deserve. The stories I share throughout this book are true stories.

Now, I'm going to share my personal perspective on belief. My perspective is that without a high level of belief in all aspects of your life, you will only reach an average level of success. My question for you here is: who really wants to just be average? Do you want more for your family? Do you want a better life? Do you want to reach your ultimate potential and success? I'm talking about your ultimate success. I'm talking about you being in the category of the top three, five or ten percent top money earners worldwide. There are some of you that just read that statement and are saying to yourself, "That's crazy! I couldn't do that! I couldn't be in the top ten percent most successful people or money earners!" Well I hate to say this but if this is what you are thinking, you are right! That is your belief system and you will remain right where you are in life.

One big difference between the most successful people in the world and you is their belief and their application of the success principles to their plan. They see their vision or goal vividly; they create a detailed, specific plan which creates their vision; they overcome every adversity as it comes along; they never quit; they continually learn and grow professionally; they work smarter and harder than everyone else; and most of all, they have 100% belief in themselves, in their vision, goal or project. They don't quit until the completion of their goal.

It's time to learn more about belief and why it is the number one principle and foundation of success. First, we will discuss self-belief. In order to create any level of success you must believe in yourself. Self-belief creates self-confidence. With self-confidence you will be able to create the vision and the plan of action to accomplish your vision. I'm not a psychologist, but I have read many books on the mind and how it works. Here is what I've learned. First your conscious mind can only hold one thought at a time. Whatever you think about or focus on is your dominant thought. Your subconscious mind can process billions of units of data at the same time. However, the dominant thought of your conscious mind is what your subconscious mind also focuses on. When the dominant thought is of your vision, goals, project, or success, your subconscious mind begins to create ideas. The subconscious then sends the ideas to your conscious mind to create the plan and put it into action.

Self-belief and self-confidence create positive thoughts that you can and will have success. Basically, what you think about consistently (your dominant thought) will happen whether it is a positive or negative thought. As an example, if you continually think, "I can't do this! This won't work!" your mind will never create a plan to move forward. Because you have already planted the thought, it won't happen. So your thought is right, it won't happen!

This is evidenced in anything and everything we do in life. Have you ever thought at work that what you are doing is hard? If that is what you are thinking, then that's what will happen. It will be hard! The same is true of your vision or goals. If you believe the vision or goals are not within reach, you won't be able to accomplish them. The reason you can't and won't accomplish the vision or goal is your mind has already stopped working on a plan because you don't believe it is possible. You give up and don't put in the necessary effort. The mind says you can't do this and its over before you even start.

This leads you to total belief in what you're doing. If you don't believe fully in your project, product, sales goals and company, you will not have the inspiration, passion, drive or desire to create success or your desired outcome. I'm not saying here that you need to be using the product. You must believe in its validity, value and ethics. Without this belief, you will not be able to share its true value or worth to those you sell to.

Belief that you deserve the success must also be present in order to create the success you desire. If you don't believe you deserve the success, the success you dream of will not come to pass. The lack of hope or desire is looking at things negatively. Your dominant thought daily is that you don't deserve the success. You don't deserve the financial freedom. You don't deserve the home of your dreams. This type of thinking stops the creative side of your subconscious. Your mind will not create a plan to accomplish your vision, goals, or success because your dominant thought has already stopped the creative process. You need to see your success. You need to see the home you deserve. You must see what your life is like with the financial status you desire and deserve. If you talk to any high level athlete, they will almost always tell you that they visualize their success before it actually happens. You must change your thinking!

VISION

Even the Bible talks about the importance of vision. In Proverb's 29:18 says, "Where there is no vision, the people will parish." These are the words of King Solomon, known as the wisest and richest man to ever live (his estimated peak wealth was 2.1 trillion in today's dollars).

In order to get where you are going in your professional or personal life, you need to know what the end destination looks like. This is your vision. Some people call it your goal. Your vision includes, every facet of your life, everything you want in life, and at what level you want to accomplish it. To set goals and to make plans, you must begin with the end in mind. That is why you must have a vision of what your success looks like. This includes where you want to live. The house you want to live in. What position you see yourself attaining at work. How much money you want to earn. What financial success you want to accomplish (amount of money in the bank). What kind of friends you want to have. Without a vision of where you want to go, you can't create the plan to get there. It would be like driving from San Diego to New York without a map or GPS.

In Napoleon Hill's classic book *Think and Grow Rich*, I read a true story about a man who stopped short of his vision. His name was R. U. Harby. He had gold fever and bought the rights to a gold mine. He worked the mine for a few years and found a vein of gold. He covered up his find and went home to raise the money for machinery needed to bring the ore to the surface. He raised the money and returned with his nephew Darby. Things started well and before long, they were able to pay back their debts. Then the vein of gold ore disappeared. After some time, they quit mining in frustration and sold their machinery to a junk man for a few hundred dollars. After they went home disappointed, the astute junk man called in a mining engineer who checked the mine and calculated that there was a vein of gold just three feet away from where R.U. Harby and Darby quit digging. The junk man went on to make millions. His strike was one of the largest veins of gold ever found in the area. Here is the key to this story. The vein of gold they hit was only 3 feet short of where the previous owner stopped digging. Whenever you feel like giving up on your vision or dreams, remember that you may be just three feet from gold. Don't stop short of your success! You could be just short of achieving your ultimate success.

INTEGRITY

There will be no success without integrity in your life. To me, integrity is the most important character trait we can establish. Integrity is all we have. It is the foundation of who we are and what we personally represent. It is also the foundation of trust with others. Without a great foundation, everything else at some point will crumble. So to reach your vision of success, help from others will be critical to have in your life.

To put this in simple terms, integrity comes from a Greek word *integer*. So let's stretch our memory and go back to high school. An integer is a whole number, right? Well lets apply that to a few analogies in life. To live with integrity is to live a truthful life. I know that we are not perfect, but when we make mistakes we need to correct them and make them right as quickly as possible. I have friends in the construction industry and they use cement for their foundations. The construction workers use the word integrity when they talk about the foundations. When a construction company pours the foundation of a building, they want the cement to have integrity. That basically means they want the foundation to have no cracks in it. That makes it a strong foundation. In our lives when we tell little lies, those are little cracks in our foundations of character. The problem starts there. The little lies then turn into bigger lies and before you know it, your foundation of integrity as a person falls apart. You lose trust from those around you. So it's almost impossible to create your vision of success without integrity because you will lose the help of those around you.

GOAL SETTING AND PLANNING

I've mentioned vision many times in this book. Goal setting and planning starts with that vision of what the end result will be. I'm referencing again from King Solomon, the wisest man in history. He said that without vision the people will parish. Without a vision, or dream there is no hope. Without belief and a plan to accomplish that vision it will remain only a dream. A lot of people dream of better times. They hope for things to get better. But most people don't have a plan to make things better. They don't do anything differently to change their current circumstances. Your vision must be the dominant thought every day.

The difference to me between a dream and your vision is knowing and believing it will happen and then creating a written plan to create that vision. Successful people see in their minds the end result of their success. Successful people will very clearly see the success before they ever start their plan. Successful people also see the end actually as the beginning. With your vision of success clearly in mind, you can then work backwards on setting time lines and short and long term goals. As an example: let's say you are a developer of commercial property. You want to build a high rise sky scraper. To start you need to know the location, the ground composition, the height allowed and other specs. You'll also have a full architectural drawing and a complete design of what it will look like when it is completed. After this and many other elements, you can put time lines to building your vision. In your success vision plan, just like in building a building, there will be daily, weekly, monthly and yearly goals in order to create the final vision or project. It doesn't matter what the final vision, goal or project is, without an action plan using daily, weekly, monthly and yearly goals, your vision of success will remain only a dream, a hope, or a wish. You must create a plan and you must take action on that plan. Remember, it all starts with the end in mind.

WORK ETHIC

Most people think they have a good work ethic. Most people think they work hard. Have you ever thought to yourself, "Man, I work harder than that guy or girl. Why are they having more success than I am?" I'm sure we have all thought this at one time or another in our lives. I know I have! The answer to this question is simple. It's not just about working harder or longer than someone else. It's more about working harder on things that matter most. Things that will bring you one step closer to your vision, success or goal.

I'm talking about the big things. Most people that don't see much success are often spending most of their time and hard work on things that need to be done but aren't as important. Those things that are not a priority to move you one step closer to your vision, success, or goal. The key is to plan your day or design your day to move toward your vision of success. I love this quote from one of my mentors, Jim Rohn, "If you don't design your life plan, chances are you'll fall into someone else's plan. And guess what they have planned for you. Not much." Basically, they are fitting you into their plan to create their success. So in designing your days and life, do the important things first. The busy work will take up most of your time and prevent you from achieving your ultimate success.

Here is my perspective about work ethic as it relates to success. Success is not an overnight phenomenon. It takes time! Sometimes it takes months, sometimes years, and for some things maybe a lifetime. To create the success, you really want and deserve, you must be willing to work as hard as it takes for as long as it takes. Be as consistent as it takes, and be as persistent as needed. Work on the things that matter the most. You must have a no quit attitude and a belief in yourself and your plan that is unfailing. Most people become discouraged and stop just short of their vision of success.

PERSONAL GROWTH &
LIFE LONG LEARNING

To create more personal success and also to sustain it, you must grow as a person. Jim Rohn, one of the biggest business and personal growth philosophers of our time, says the following, "You need to work harder on yourself than you do on your job." If you don't improve, change and become a better person, you will not have the huge success you want and deserve. More importantly, you will not be able to sustain your success. It will go away!

Another one of my mentors, Chris Widener, in his book *Art of Influence*, discusses this topic as well. He talks about the fact that most people don't pick up a book and read after they finish high school or college. You need to read books, listen to CD's or go to seminars that help you improve yourself personally. I believe fully that the people that do this have a leg up on their competition. Your competition won't be taking the time to do this. This is something that we all need to be doing for our lifetime. What better pursuit is there than to become a better person, a better husband and father, a better employee, employer or leader of others.

I'm sure you have heard stories of regular middle class people and even people that come from the poverty level winning the lottery. They win millions of dollars and according to the National Endowment for Financial Services, 70% of them are broke again within a few years. In a Sports Illustrated article it shared that 78% of ex-NFL players are bankrupt or in serious financial problems. In the NBA 60% of the players have these same issues. These professional athletes make millions of dollars playing their sport. They make even more on their endorsements. The fact remains that the majority of them are broke after a few years of retiring from sports.

The reason this happens to these individuals is that they still have a broke mind set. These people didn't grow personally and are not mentally responsible or equal to their recent financial status. The broke mindset they grew up with has not changed just because they now have money. They don't have the belief that they deserve the money. This really boils down to their personal growth level and their belief system in themselves and money. A lot of people grew up with the Bible and actually believe that money is the root of all evil. In the Bible it doesn't state this. It actually says that "the love of money is the root of all evil." This literally means that you put money ahead of all else. This belief system, the lack of personal growth, along with belief that you don't deserve the money is what keeps people financially unsuccessful.

- What are you listening to

    - In your car?

    - When you work out?

    - When you go for a walk?

    - Street biking or mountain biking?

    - Watching television?

- Is what you are listening to improving you personally or bringing you closer to your goal or success? You need to constantly feed your mind positive, personal growth information to change the way you think. Change your thinking, change your circumstances.

- The average American:

    - Drives 12,000 - 15,000 miles, this is a minimum of 300-400 hours annually in the car

    - Walks, bikes or engages in sports activities 650 hours annually

    - Watches television, 1,716 hours annually

- If you listen to a good book, training or something inspirational you could improve yourself and in turn improve your life. Using this much time wisely would give you a PHD in self-education.

"An education will make you a living, a self-education will make you a fortune."

~Jim Rohn

OVERCOMING ADVERSITY

People in the world today and throughout time have created their visions of success to the highest degree. Are those people who have the belief, the vision, the plan, and a no quit attitude? The top three, five and ten percent money earners are the people who were willing to go through any adversity, any obstacle, and do whatever it takes to create their success. You know the kind of people I'm talking about. People like Donald Trump, Bill Gates, Steve Jobs, Darren Hardy (CEO of Success Magazine), Phil Knight of Nike, Abraham Lincoln, Martin Luther King Jr. (by the way, Martin Luther King Jr.'s famous speech started with *I believe*, then he took action), and many others.

I know what you're probably thinking, that these people didn't have any real problems. Did these people start with money or just got lucky? It's been interesting for me in life. The harder I've worked, the luckier I have been. I know from studying successful people like those mentioned above and many others, the same is true of them as well. Highly successful individuals have overcome more adversity than we have. In fact, the more successful an individual is, the more adversity they have overcome. "The bigger the success, the bigger the problems are that you have to overcome." That's the difference! Highly successful individuals have also failed many, many, many more times than most people. Did I say many? The difference between these successful people and everyone else is how they handle the adversity and failure. What they learn from it. What they did differently moving forward based on what they learned.

I was at a training seminar where Donald Trump was the key note speaker. He was training on success principles. In this training, Mr. Trump told a personal story about what happened to him financially in the early nineties. Mr. Trump had basically lost everything because of the collapse of the economy. At that time, he was highly leveraged with his commercial building projects. Mr. Trump found himself going from approximately six billion in the black to one billion in debt. Mr. Trump told us that during this time, he and his wife were walking down the streets of Manhattan and came across a homeless man. Mr. Trump turned to his wife and said that this homeless man is worth about a billion dollars more than we are right now.

The reason I share this story with you is this was a huge obstacle for him to overcome. He had to make a choice on where to go from there. Mr. Trump, like all highly successful people, had an unshakable belief in himself, in his vision, and in his plans to accomplish his vision. Mr. Trump during this time was scheduled to attend a black tie affair. Some of the bankers that he owed money to were going to be in attendance at this event. He told us that he was thinking about not attending the event, but finally decided to go anyway.

As fate would have it, he was seated right next to one of the bankers he owed money to. In fact, I believe this individual was one that he owed the most money to. During the evening they talked. A personal relationship and mutual respect was built. Before the evening was over, they had set up a meeting for the next week to discuss the debt owed. During that meeting they worked out the details of a plan to pay the debt back. Because of Mr. Trump facing this adversity, he overcame the financial failure.

Today Mr. Trump has the biggest financial comeback in history (according to *The Guinness Book of Records*). He went from a billion in debt to over eight billion in the black. When you are looking at your problems or failures, reflect on this story. Highly successful people truly believe in their vision, plans and success. So the adversity or failure, no matter how big, becomes just a bump on the road to success. Remember the road to success will be filled with adversity, problems and failures. Your success depends on how you handle them and keep moving forward.

This comes back to how much you believe in yourself, in your vision, and in your plan. I often listen to a CD training in my car from Jim Rohn, *Building Your Networking Marketing Business*. It talks about adversity. In that training, Mr. Rohn goes through something called the "Set of Your Sail." I think you will like this analogy,

> The winds of circumstance blow upon all of us. We all have experienced the winds of disappointment, despair and heartbreak, but why do people arrive at such different places at the end of the journey? Have we all not sailed upon the same sea? The major difference isn't the circumstances; it's the set of the sail, or the way we think. In spite of our best efforts, we have moments when things just seem to fall apart. The rich and the poor have the same challenges that can lead to financial ruin and personal despair. It isn't what happens to us that determines the quality of our lives. It's what we do after we've set our sails and the wind decides to change direction. When winds change, we must change. We have to struggle to our feet and reset the sail in a manner that will steer us to the direction of our deliberate choice. The set of the sail, how we think and how we respond, has a far greater capacity to destroy our lives than any challenges we face. How quickly we respond to adversity is far more important than adversity itself. The great challenge of life is to control the process of our own thinking. Your personal philosophy is the greatest determining factor in how your life works out.

What Jim Rohn says about the set of the sail is exactly what Mr. Trump and many highly successful people use to overcome adversity.

You may have heard this story about Thomas Edison. In his lifetime, he is credited for 2,332 worldwide patents and 1093 US patents. He is most known for the invention of the light bulb and energy. He is also credited for the phonograph, recorded sound, telegraph, batteries, and many other inventions. After he had succeeded in creating the light bulb, he was interviewed. The interviewer asked him how it felt to have failed over 10,000 times before he succeeded in inventing the light bulb? His reply was interesting! He said "I have failed 10,000 times? I just found 10,000 ways that won't work." Obviously, he just kept moving forward, learned from his mistakes and created success.

More proof of people that overcome adversity: I want to share this about Abraham Lincoln. This is probably one of my favorite stories. Most of you know Abraham Lincoln as one of our greatest presidents. What most people don't know is the struggle and adversity he went through prior to becoming president. Here are the dates and failures he went through before finally succeeding.

1832 – He lost his job and was defeated for state legislature.

1833 – His business failed.

1835 – His sweetheart died.

1836 – He had a nervous breakdown.

1838 – Defeated for Speaker.

1843 – Defeated for nomination for Congress.

1848 – Lost renomination for Congress.

1849 – Rejected for Land Officer.

1854 – Defeated for US Senate.

1856 – Defeated for the nomination for Vice President.

1858 – Defeated for US Senate.

1860 – Elected President of the United States.

- The question here is how far are you willing to go?

- What are you willing to overcome to create your success?

AFFILIATIONS

The people you spend the most time with have a huge impact on your success. Jim Rohn believes, "You are the average of the five people you spend the most time with." This being said, don't you think it is important to evaluate who you're spending time with? I believe your affiliations are very important to help you reach your vision of success. I'm not saying here that you need to give up your current friends. What I'm saying for certain is that you need to add some new friends to the circle. If you want more success in life, you need to spend time with people that are more successful than you. That is where you can listen, learn and emulate people that have a life that you want. These are the people that will help you get to your vision of success in life.

In many of the stories I shared, you heard a common theme that surrounding yourself with successful people has helped the individuals create success. All the stories I shared are friends of mine and the types of people I've surrounded myself with. As a result of my affiliations, my friends have helped me in the past and continue to help me create my success today.

WELL-ROUNDED LIFE (BODY, SOUL & SPIRIT)

The importance of a well-rounded life is that it helps you live a happier, more complete life personally. Living healthy will not just help you live longer, but you will feel better and look better. So take care of yourself with exercise and eating properly. This is also taking care of your personal relationships. Take time to spend with your family and friends. This helps you mentally and physically to be at your best. It also builds stronger relationships with those close to you. Remember, the work you don't complete will be there tomorrow. The time you miss out on with family and friends you can never get it back. You can't make it up and before you know it, the kids are gone and friends have moved away. The old saying that time is money, is wrong. Time is more precious than money. You can make more money but you can never get your time back. So spend your time wisely.

The last part I want to discuss is spirituality. I'm not talking here about going to church and hitting people over the head with your Bible. We are all spiritual beings and whatever you pursue here, it is a vital part of you as a person. If you think about some of the greatest leaders in history, they had a strong spiritual side to them. People like

Buddha, Aristotle, Christopher Columbus, Galileo, George Washington, Orville and Wilbur Wright, Napoleon Bonaparte, Martin Luther King Jr., Gandhi, Mother Teresa, Abraham Lincoln, and many others. The interesting thing about most of these leaders is that they all had belief in their causes. That helped them all become the great people we know them as today. The fact remains that many of the great and successful people in the world have a strong spiritual side. Working on these three areas helps you become well rounded as a person.

COMMUNICATION & LISTENING SKILLS

This book continues to be about accomplishing your success. Having good communication and listening skills is another principle needed to create your success. In order for you to create your success, you need to create a written plan. A written plan is your written communication skills. To take action on your plan, you will need to have others help you to get there. You will also need to be able to communicate your plan and vision verbally to others.

Also, you need to have good listening skills. This will help you learn from those more successful than you. A big stumbling block for many of us is that we don't have the humility to know what we don't know. We don't want the help needed from others to reach our vision. We can all learn something from others. God gave us two ears and one mouth. Use them accordingly. These communication tips will help you reach your vision of success.

HUMILITY

Humility is a character trait that is of utmost importance to sustain your success. In the Bible, Proverbs 16:18, King Solomon wrote, "Pride goes before destruction, and a haughty spirit before a fall." My advice to being humble is that you need to keep a grateful spirit. Be thankful for what you have and what you accomplish. Without the help of others and, in my belief, the help of God, we couldn't accomplish anything. So there is no reason for any of us to be boastful. No one wants to be around anyone who is full of themselves and thinks they know everything or thinks they did everything themselves. There are those who think humility is a weakness. The reality is that humility is a strength.

EXCELLENCE

The definition of excellence is the quality of being outstanding or extremely good. To create your success you will need help from other people. You are either attracting people to you or you are repelling people. Being an individual of excellence helps you attract that help. Some of you may remember a show called *Life Styles of the Rich and Famous*. This and other reality shows portrayed life styles of people that lived a life of excellence. They were successful, wealthy, and we all wanted to be them.

There are a few areas of your life that encompass excellence and help attract people into your world. The first is your personal appearance, which is the first impression people have of you. The saying,

"A first impression is a lasting impression," is so true. I'm not saying you need to wear a suit everyday or be a male or female model. I am saying that you need to look the best you can with a neat, clean, sharp appearance. According to the definition of excellence, being the best is not just about appearance. It's about doing the best job you can do. My father always said that if something is worth doing, it's worth doing right. Take pride in the person you are. Take pride in your work and in yourself.

- What is the most important skill or trait you need to develop to achieve your desired success?

    - Belief?

    - Communication skills?

    - Leadership/Influence?

    - Time management?

    - Consistency?

    - Persistence?

    - Discipline?

CHAPTER SEVEN
FINAL THOUGHTS

This book was written for the sole purpose of sharing my personal story and stories of other successful people I know, in hopes that you can find belief in yourself. If I can have a start in life which would be considered much lower than most and reach a fairly high level of success, my belief is that everyone can have whatever success in life they believe in and choose to reach. Each and every one of you that commit to your dream can accomplish it. You can live the life you have always wanted to live. The only thing you need to do is to make a decision that you are going to do it and do it now. You need to take some time and figure out what you really want out of life. Once you have a crystal clear vision of the dream and goal, you must commit to it. You must believe beyond a shadow of a doubt that you can and will accomplish your goal. This belief will allow your mind to create a step-by-step written plan to accomplish your goal. Figure out who you need help from to accomplish your goals and start taking action. I say again, start taking action. Without taking action each day toward your goal, you can't get there. All it takes is consistent effort over a long enough period of time and you can get there. I can't guarantee how long it will take, that's up to you. I can guarantee that if you don't start, you will never get there.

I have faith in each and every one of you that are reading this book, because you obviously want something else, something better for your life. I want to share with you a number of books that I have read that have inspired me. I think these books will help you understand more about what I have written here. They will help you grow personally and professionally and add to what I have shared with you. I hope you all enjoyed reading my story of success as well as those of some of my friends. I know it wasn't glamorous, but it does show what can be accomplished when you truly believe.

Reaching success is a process which consists of applying all the success principles I have shared. You also have to incorporate constant personal growth into your daily life. The more you grow personally the more confidence you will have. The more influence you will have with others. The more belief you will gain in yourself. Some of the books I have read that have really impacted my life and my success are: *The Art of Influence* and *Above All Else* by Chris Widener, *The Compound Affect* by Darren Hardy, *Developing the Leader Within You* and *Developing the Leaders Around You* by John Maxwell, *How to Win Friends and Influence People* by Dale Carnegie, *Think and Grow Rich* by Napoleon Hill, *12 Pillars* by Jim Rohn and Chris Widener, *The Traveler's Gift* and *Final Summit* by Andy Andrews, *The Resilient Power of Purpose* and *Overcoming Objections Will Make you Rich* by Larry Di-Angi, *Go For No* by Richard Fenton, and *Above and Beyond the Rim* by my friend Joe Courtney (NBA star).

To end this book, I want to say that we all have choices every day that shape our lives. Some are as simple as should I make one more sales call? Small decisions and choices make a huge impact over time. Some decisions are big ones, like where should I go to college?

What job should I take? Should I get married? Should I have kids or buy a house? Should I be dishonest? Should I tell a lie? Every choice we make should be made based on belief in ourselves, our belief system and whether or not it's taking me where I want to go in life. Every choice, big and small, changes the course of our lives in one direction or another. I can't remember who told me this but POOR stands for *passing over opportunities regularly.* Don't let that happen to you. Remember, as Jim Rohn says, "You can't change your destination overnight, but you can change you direction overnight." And to follow with Lou Burgess, "Nothing will work unless you do." Remember this!

My hope for all of you that have read this book is that you make a choice to change your belief in yourself and belief in your plan for your future success. You can have the life you want to live but you must first believe it.

ACTION PLAN

1. Take time and crystalize your goals, vision or dreams.

   a. Set aside time alone and really think about what your best life looks like, then write it down.

      i. The job you want.

      ii. The money you want to make.

      iii. Where you want to live.

      iv.   How much money you want in the bank.

2.   Create a written plan with timelines to accomplish your vision, goals and dreams.

      a.   What resources will you need?

      b.   What people will you need to help you?

      c.   What is your time table to reach your vision, goals or dreams?

      d.   Create daily, weekly, monthly and yearly goals.

      e.   Evaluate your plan weekly or monthly and change direction when necessary.

3.   Take action today and everyday toward your goal.

      a.   The compound effect of small steps over time creates your success.

      b.   Be committed.

      c.   Be consistent.

      d.   Be persistent.

      e.   Maintain a no quit attitude.

4.   Repeat.

ABOUT GARY

 Gary Varnell has 35 years of Corporate Business experience and business ownership experience. He has experience and success at all levels in business, sales, sales management, sales training, public speaking and C-level management. Gary has been a speaker and trainer since 1989. He has shared the stage with professional athletes, best-selling authors and top business executives. He has spoken to small and large groups and is very passionate about delivering information, concepts and action steps to help individuals, sales teams, entrepreneurial groups, and companies go to a higher level of success. Gary speaks on success principles, leadership, sales, goal setting and planning. The information Gary delivers is designed to change the thinking or mindset of people and inspire them to take immediate action to facilitate powerful change.

**"If you change your mindset, you can
change the world around you."**

CPSIA information can be obtained
at www.ICGtesting.com
Printed in the USA
FSOW02n1435110216
16792FS

9 781613 398548